Presented to

_____

By

_____

On the Occasion of

_____

Date

_____

TOP 100
BIBLE VERSES
TO MEMORIZE

STRENGTHEN YOUR FAITH,
GAIN HOPE, LOVE, PEACE, AND WISDOM

STEVEN ANDREW

TOP 100
BIBLE VERSES
TO MEMORIZE

STRENGTHEN YOUR FAITH,
GAIN HOPE, LOVE, PEACE, AND WISDOM

STEVEN ANDREW

Acts One Eight Publishing

ISBN 978-0-9600149-3-4

December 2024

Published by ACTS ONE EIGHT Publishing™

Also available as eBook: ISBN 978-0-9600149-2-7

Contents

ھے

Preface

∾

This book of hope that you are reading, the "Top 100 Bible Verses to Memorize," can be used your whole life. God will encourage you and provide help for your needs. These Scriptures can give you wisdom, make peace in relationships, bring the Lord's forgiveness, give you God's victory in battles, prevent wrong decisions, and save souls.

Everything you need in life is in the Word of God. Do you want to know God better? Do you desire His peace, love, truth, power, and wisdom? Would you like to live the victorious Christian life? Memorizing these key 100 Bible verses will give you God's help and answers. Additionally, these promises from God will help you walk faithfully with the Lord. Imagine how much better your life will be with these promises of God!

Everyone, no matter their age, can memorize a Bible verse each week. You can keep this book with you all your life. It is important to have the "Top 100 Bible Verses to Memorize" for yourself and to give a copy to every loved one. Who would benefit from this book? Family members? A classroom? A group? A church? Do you want to change lives? Imagine if every child had this book and memorized a Bible verse each week?

As a pastor for over 30 years, I have experience helping people and families with their needs. That is why I prayerfully selected these important 100 Bible verses to assist you. They are arranged in an order that provides a

Biblical foundation for important areas of your life. My prayer is that you memorize these 100 verses and know God better. If you want more Scriptures, there is a bonus of 100 additional Bible verses included in the second chapter. The third chapter is for writing other Scriptures you memorize. This way, all your memorized Bible verses are in one place.

The "Top 100 Bible Verses to Memorize" also contains a Bible Promise Book! This fourth chapter has the same verses arranged by topics. The verse numbers in the Promise Book match the verse numbers in the first part. You have a life-changing journey as you learn these promises from God.

After the Holy Bible, this powerful little book, the "Top 100 Bible Verses to Memorize," can be your most important book to have. You can live with God's wisdom. There is always hope, love, and answers for you in God's Word!

Tips to Boost Memorization

What is the best way to quickly and effectively memorize Bible verses?

Some people memorize phrase by phrase. They start with the first few words and the reference, then gradually add more words until the entire verse is memorized. Repeating the verse three times a day helps some people. Others may write down the Bible verse multiple times daily until it is committed to memory. Analytical individuals might use flashcards, while creative ones could set the verse to music.

Another effective method is memorizing verses together as a family, with friends, or within a church group. You can recite a verse before dinner, during a church service, or on a phone call. You might also create a quiz by asking, "What is this verse?" and giving the reference for others to answer. What is the easiest way for you to memorize?

One way I memorize verses is while exercising. For example, I do a set of weights, and during the rest period before the next set, I quote a Bible verse from memory and check if I recited it correctly. Another method I use is to sit and go through verses one at a time.

There is a circle checkbox by each Bible verse to mark when you have memorized it. You can review each verse you memorize by reading the Bible reference out loud, like "John 3:16." Then, look away and quote the verse from memory. Afterward, check in the book to see if you quoted the verse correctly. You can also write the date you memorize the verse next to the checkbox.

Setting a goal can be helpful. I recommend memorizing one Bible verse per week. Can you do it? Or perhaps you prefer to memorize a new Scripture every two or three days. Never give up. Keep at this and your life will change.

I am praying for you. Love in Christ,

Steven Andrew
Pastor, USA Christian Church

ॐ Sign up for my email at USA.Church and stay updated.
ॐ Follow me on USA.Life Christian social network.

Prayer of Salvation

Our greatest need is salvation by calling on Jesus Christ to save us. Here is a prayer:

Father, You, Lord, are the one true God. I want to be a Christian. I believe Jesus Christ died on the cross to forgive my sins. I believe You raised Jesus Christ from the dead. Jesus is Lord. Help me understand the Bible as I read Your Word. In Jesus' name. Amen.

To grow strong as a Christian, read the Bible morning and evening as you pray and seek God daily. Memorizing these verses will make a difference and bring yGod's blessings!

᪡

Scriptures are from the King James Version (KJV), which is the most popular Bible that people read. Both adults and children find the KJV easy to memorize, because it uses simple and correct words. The KJV is God's preserved Word. For accuracy and to help people understand, the KJV uses older English. For example, "ye" and "you" are plural when talking to a group. "Ye" can be "you all". This is needed to know who the verse is about. Using "ye" we know it is you plural and the translation is not lost. "Thou," "thy," "thee" and "thine" are singular for "you" when talking to one person. In other words, the "Ys" are plural and the "Ts" are singular. The KJV is the correct translation. For example, John 3:3, John 3:7, Deuteronomy 6:14-15 and other verses have the correct plural and singular in the KJV to help you understand the text correctly. If a word ends in "eth," such as "believeth," we know it is "believes". English spellings such as "neighbour" are "neighbor". These tips make it easy to understand. One reason why Americans love the KJV is, after replacing the earlier Geneva Bible, the King James Bible is the "rock" of God's Word that America is built upon.

Top 100 Bible Verses to Memorize

‿

In the beginning God created the heaven and the earth.
Genesis 1:1
1. O

For all have sinned, and come short of the glory of God;
Romans 3:23
2. O

For the wages of sin is death; but the gift of God
is eternal life through Jesus Christ our Lord.
Romans 6:23 3. O

For God so loved the world, that he gave his only begotten
Son, that whosoever believeth in him should not perish,
but have everlasting life. *Jesus Christ, John 3:16*
4. O

The LORD is gracious, and full of compassion;
slow to anger, and of great mercy.
Psalm 145:8
5. O

I am the way, the truth, and the life:
no man cometh unto the Father, but by me.
Jesus Christ, John 14:6
6. O

If we confess our sins, he is faithful and just to forgive us
our sins, and to cleanse us from all unrighteousness.
1 John 1:9
7. O

**Except a man be born again,
he cannot see the kingdom of God.**
Jesus Christ, John 3:3
8. O

**... my God shall supply all your need
according to his riches in glory by Christ Jesus.**
Philippians 4:19 9. O

I can do all things through Christ ...
Philippians 4:13 10. O

**For God hath not given us the spirit of fear;
but of power, and of love, and of a sound mind.**
2 Timothy 1:7
11. O

Children, obey your parents in the Lord: for this is right.
Ephesians 6:1 12. O

2 **Honour thy father and mother;
(which is the first commandment with promise;)**
3 **That it may be well with thee,
and thou mayest live long on the earth.**
Ephesians 6:2-3
13. O   14. O

Be ye holy; for I am holy.
1 Peter 1:16 15. O

**Being confident of this very thing,
that he which hath begun a good work in you
will perform it until the day of Jesus Christ:**
Philippians 1:6
16. O

Be still, and know that I am God:
Psalm 46:10

17. O

Submit yourselves therefore to God.
Resist the devil, and he will flee from you.
James 4:7

18. O

I am the light of the world: he that followeth me
shall not walk in darkness, but shall have the light of life.
Jesus Christ, John 8:12

19. O

I will never leave thee, nor forsake thee.
Hebrews 13:5

20. O

5 **Trust in the LORD with all thine heart;**
and lean not unto thine own understanding.
6 **In all thy ways acknowledge him,**
and he shall direct thy paths.
Proverbs 3:5-6

21. O   22. O

And be ye kind one to another, tenderhearted,
forgiving one another, even as God for Christ's sake hath
forgiven you.
Ephesians 4:32

23. O

For I the LORD thy God will hold thy right hand,
saying unto thee, Fear not; I will help thee.
Isaiah 41:13

24. O

Blessed is the nation whose God is the LORD ...
Psalm 33:12
25. O

22 **But the fruit of the Spirit is love, joy, peace,
longsuffering, gentleness, goodness, faith,**
23 **meekness, temperance:
against such there is no law.**
Galatians 5:22-23
26. O 27. O

... he hath made us accepted in the beloved.
Ephesians 1:6
28. O

He restoreth my soul:
Psalm 23:3
29. O

**He healeth the broken in heart,
and bindeth up their wounds.**
Psalm 147:3
30. O

**Likewise reckon ye also yourselves to be dead indeed unto
sin, but alive unto God through Jesus Christ our Lord.**
Romans 6:11
31. O

**And when ye stand praying, forgive,
if ye have ought against any: that your Father also
which is in heaven may forgive you your trespasses.**
Jesus Christ, Mark 11:25
32. O

... whatsoever things are true, whatsoever things are
honest, whatsoever things are just, whatsoever things are
pure, whatsoever things are lovely, whatsoever things are
of good report; if there be any virtue, and
if there be any praise, think on these things.
Philippians 4:8

33. O

30 ... Sirs, what must I do to be saved?
31 And they said, Believe on the Lord Jesus Christ,
and thou shalt be saved, and thy house.
Acts 16:30-31

34. O   35. O

I am crucified with Christ: nevertheless, I live;
yet not I, but Christ liveth in me: and the life which I now
live in the flesh I live by the faith of the Son of God,
who loved me, and gave himself for me.
Galatians 2:20

36. O

I am the resurrection, and the life:
he that believeth in me,
though he were dead, yet shall he live:
Jesus Christ, John 11:25

37. O

There hath no temptation taken you but such as is
common to man: but God is faithful, who will not suffer
you to be tempted above that ye are able;
but will with the temptation also make a way to escape,
that ye may be able to bear it.
1 Corinthians 10:13

38. O

15

**Thou wilt keep him in perfect peace, whose mind is stayed
on thee: because he trusteth in thee.**
Isaiah 26:3
39. O

**Let your light so shine before men,
that they may see your good works,
and glorify your Father which is in heaven.**
Jesus Christ, Matthew 5:16
40. O

**There is therefore now no condemnation
to them which are in Christ Jesus,
who walk not after the flesh, but after the Spirit.**
Romans 8:1 41. O

⁂

**Be strong and of a good courage; be not afraid,
neither be thou dismayed: for the LORD thy God is with
thee whithersoever thou goest.**
Joshua 1:9 42. O

**My little children, these things write I unto you, that ye sin
not. And if any man sin, we have an advocate with the
Father, Jesus Christ the righteous:**
1 John 2:1 43. O

**9 That if thou shalt confess with thy mouth the Lord Jesus,
and shalt believe in thine heart that God hath raised him
from the dead, thou shalt be saved.
10 For with the heart man believeth unto righteousness;
and with the mouth confession is made unto salvation.**
Romans 10:9-10 44. O   45. O

... they entered into a covenant to seek the LORD God
of their fathers with all their heart
and with all their soul;
2 Chronicles 15:12

46. O

... let every man be swift to hear,
slow to speak, slow to wrath:
James 1:19

47. O

If my people, which are called by my name,
shall humble themselves, and pray, and seek my face,
and turn from their wicked ways;
then will I hear from heaven, and will forgive their sin,
and will heal their land.
2 Chronicles 7:14

48. O

The fear of the LORD is the beginning of wisdom: and the
knowledge of the holy is understanding.
Proverbs 9:10

49. O

If any of you lack wisdom, let him ask of God,
that giveth to all men liberally,
and upbraideth not; and it shall be given him.
James 1:5

50. O

Wives, submit yourselves unto your own husbands,
as unto the Lord.
Ephesians 5:22

51. O

Husbands, love your wives, even as Christ also loved the church, and gave himself for it;
Ephesians 5:25

52. O

Thou shalt not lie with mankind, as with womankind: it is abomination.
Leviticus 18:22

53. O

Train up a child in the way he should go: and when he is old, he will not depart from it.
Proverbs 22:6

54. O

We ought to obey God rather than men.
Acts 5:29

55. O

For the LORD is our judge, the LORD is our lawgiver, the LORD is our king; he will save us.
Isaiah 33:22

56. O

And thou shalt love the Lord thy God with all thy heart, and with all thy soul, and with all thy mind, and with all thy strength: this is the first commandment.
First Commandment, Jesus Christ, Mark 12:30

57. O

And the second is like, namely this, Thou shalt love thy neighbour as thyself.
Second Commandment, Jesus Christ, Mark 12:31

58. O

... provide out of all the people able men,
such as fear God, men of truth, hating covetousness;
and place such over them, to be rulers...
Exodus 18:21
59. O

He that ruleth over men must be just,
ruling in the fear of God.
2 Samuel 23:3 *60. O*

But they that wait upon the LORD shall renew their
strength; they shall mount up with wings as eagles;
they shall run, and not be weary;
and they shall walk, and not faint.
Isaiah 40:31 *61. O*

... the truth shall make you free.
John 8:32 *62. O*

These things have I written unto you that believe on the
name of the Son of God; that ye may know that ye have
eternal life, and that ye may believe on the name of the
Son of God.
1 John 5:13
63. O

... with God all things are possible.
Jesus Christ, Mark 10:27 *64. O*

... when they began to sing and to praise,
the LORD set ambushments against
the children of Ammon, Moab, and mount Seir,
which were come against Judah; and they were smitten.
2 Chronicles 20:22 *65. O*

**And whatsoever ye do, do it heartily,
as to the Lord, and not unto men;**
Colossians 3:23

66. O

**For thou shalt worship no other god:
for the LORD, whose name is Jealous, is a jealous God:**
Exodus 34:14

67. O

&

**But seek ye first the kingdom of God, and his
righteousness; and all these things
shall be added unto you.**
Matthew 6:33

68. O

**And we know that all things work together
for good to them that love God...**
Romans 8:28

69. O

**Put on the whole armour of God, that ye may be able
to stand against the wiles of the devil.**
Ephesians 6:11

70. O

**For we wrestle not against flesh and blood, but against
principalities, against powers, against the rulers of the
darkness of this world, against spiritual wickedness
in high places.**
Ephesians 6:12

71. O

14 **Stand therefore, having your loins girt about with truth,**
and having on the breastplate of righteousness;
15 **And your feet shod with the preparation**
of the gospel of peace;
16 **Above all, taking the shield of faith, wherewith ye shall**
be able to quench all the fiery darts of the wicked.
17 **And take the helmet of salvation,**
and the sword of the Spirit, which is the word of God:
18 **Praying always with all prayer and supplication**
in the Spirit, and watching thereunto with all perseverance
and supplication for all saints;
Ephesians 6:14-18
72. O   73. O   74. O   75. O   76. O

But the Comforter, which is the Holy Ghost, whom the
Father will send in my name, he shall teach you all things,
and bring all things to your remembrance, whatsoever I
have said unto you.
Jesus Christ, John 14:26
77. O

... where the Spirit of the Lord is, there is liberty.
2 Corinthians 3:17
78. O

... the glorious liberty of the children of God.
Romans 8:21
79. O

8 **For by grace are ye saved through faith;**
and that not of yourselves: it is the gift of God:
9 **Not of works, lest any man should boast.**
Ephesians 2:8- 9
80. O   81. O

21

The woman shall not wear that which pertaineth unto a
man, neither shall a man put on a woman's garment:
for all that do so are abomination unto the LORD thy God.
Deuteronomy 22:5
82. O

The thief cometh not, but for to steal, and to kill,
and to destroy: I am come that they might have life,
and that they might have it more abundantly.
John 10:10
83. O

... for I am the LORD that healeth thee.
Exodus 15:26 84. O

... by whose stripes ye were healed.
1 Peter 2:24
85. O

But without faith it is impossible to please him:
for he that cometh to God must believe that he is,
and that he is a rewarder of them that diligently seek him.
Hebrews 11:6
86. O

Blessed are the peacemakers:
for they shall be called the children of God.
Jesus Christ, Matthew 5:9
87. O

For ye have not received the spirit of bondage again to
fear; but ye have received the Spirit of adoption,
whereby we cry, Abba, Father.
Romans 8:15
88. O

... whosoever shall say unto this mountain,
Be thou removed, and be thou cast into the sea; and shall
not doubt in his heart, but shall believe that those things
which he saith shall come to pass; he shall have
whatsoever he saith.
Jesus Christ, Mark 11:23 89. O

What things soever ye desire, when ye pray,
believe that ye receive them, and ye shall have them.
Jesus Christ, Mark 11:24 90. O

10 There shall not be found among you any one that
maketh his son or his daughter to pass through the fire, or
that useth divination, or an observer of times,
or an enchanter, or a witch,
11 or a charmer, or a consulter with familiar spirits,
or a wizard, or a necromancer.
12 For all that do these things are an abomination unto the
LORD: and because of these abominations the LORD thy
God doth drive them out from before thee.
Deuteronomy 18:10-12
91. O   92 O   93. O

Delight thyself also in the LORD;
and he shall give thee the desires of thine heart.
Psalm 37:4 94. O

And the king stood in his place, and made a covenant
before the LORD, to walk after the LORD, and to keep his
commandments, and his testimonies, and his statutes,
with all his heart, and with all his soul, to perform the
words of the covenant which are written in this book.
2 Chronicles 34:31 95. O

23

As for me, this *is* my covenant with them, saith the LORD;
My spirit that *is* upon thee, and my words which I have put
in thy mouth, shall not depart out of thy mouth, nor out of
the mouth of thy seed, nor out of the mouth of thy seed's
seed, saith the LORD, from henceforth and for ever.
Isaiah 59:21
96. O

This book of the law shall not depart out of thy mouth;
but thou shalt meditate therein day and night,
that thou mayest observe to do according to all that is
written therein: for then thou shalt make thy way
prosperous, and then thou shalt have good success.
Joshua 1:8
97. O

❧

9 Because thou hast made the LORD, which is my refuge,
even the most High, thy habitation;
10 There shall no evil befall thee,
neither shall any plague come nigh thy dwelling.
Psalm 91:9-10 98. O   99. O

... as for me and my house, we will serve the LORD.
Joshua 24:15
100. O

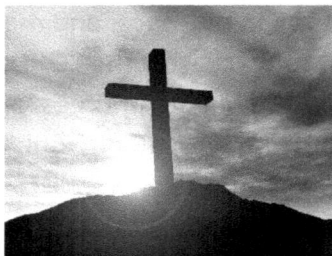

Bonus 100 Bible Verses

⨏

God cares for you. Here are additional Scriptures for your life to know. You can memorize these verses too if desired.

For we walk by faith, not by sight:
2 Corinthians 5:7
101. O

Pray without ceasing.
1 Thessalonians 5:17
102. O

**Now the God of hope fill you with all joy and peace
in believing, that ye may abound in hope,
through the power of the Holy Ghost.**
Romans 15:13
103. O

Casting all your care upon him; for he careth for you.
1 Peter 5:7
104. O

**Fear not: for they that be with us
are more than they that be with them.**
2 Kings 6:16 105. O

**If it be possible, as much as lieth in you,
live peaceably with all men.**
Romans 12:18
106. O

**Now faith is the substance of things hoped for,
the evidence of things not seen.** *Hebrews 11:1*
107. O

**Therefore if any man be in Christ,
he is a new creature: old things are passed away;
behold, all things are become new.**
2 Corinthians 5:17 108. O

**Ask, and it shall be given you; seek, and ye shall find;
knock, and it shall be opened unto you:**
Jesus Christ, *Matthew 7:7*
109. O

... the LORD hath sought him a man after his own heart ...
1 Samuel 13:14
110. O

**And now abideth faith, hope, charity, these three;
but the greatest of these *is* charity.**
1 Corinthians 13:13 111. O

**Come unto me, all ye that labour
and are heavy laden, and I will give you rest.**
Matthew 11:28
112. O

16 **All scripture is given by inspiration of God,
and is profitable for doctrine, for reproof,
for correction, for instruction in righteousness:**
17 **That the man of God may be perfect,
throughly furnished unto all good works.**
2 Timothy 3:16-17
113. O   114. O

**For in the time of trouble he shall hide me
in his pavilion: in the secret of his tabernacle
shall he hide me; he shall set me up upon a rock.**
Psalm 27:5 115. O

**Let no corrupt communication proceed out of your mouth,
but that which is good to the use of edifying,
that it may minister grace unto the hearers.**
Ephesians 4:29
116. O

**Let the words of my mouth, and the meditation of my
heart, be acceptable in thy sight, O LORD,
my strength, and my redeemer.**
Psalm 19:14 117. O

**Thy word have I hid in mine heart,
that I might not sin against thee.**
Psalm 119:11 118. O

6 **Be careful for nothing; but in every thing
by prayer and supplication with thanksgiving
let your requests be made known unto God.**
7 **And the peace of God, which passeth all understanding,
shall keep your hearts and minds through Christ Jesus.**
Philippians 4:6-7
119. O   120. O

14 **And this is the confidence that we have in him,
that, if we ask any thing according to his will,
he heareth us:**
15 **And if we know that he hear us, whatsoever we ask,
we know that we have the petitions
that we desired of him.**
1 John 5:14-15
121. O   122. O

For the love of money is the root of all evil:
1 Timothy 6:10 123. O

Ten Commandments

I am the LORD thy God ...
Exodus 20:2

Preface of our Lawgiver   124. O

Thou shalt have no other gods before me.
Exodus 20:3

First Commandment   125. O

4 Thou shalt not make unto thee any graven image, or any likeness of any thing that is in heaven above, or that is in the earth beneath, or that is in the water under the earth: 5 Thou shalt not bow down thyself to them, nor serve them: for I the LORD thy God am a jealous God...
Exodus 20:4-5

Second Commandment   126. O   127. O

Thou shalt not take the name of the LORD thy God in vain; for the LORD will not hold him guiltless that taketh his name in vain.
Exodus 20:7

Third Commandment   128. O

8 Remember the sabbath day, to keep it holy.
Exodus 20:8

Fourth Commandment   129. O

Honour thy father and thy mother: that thy days may be long upon the land which the LORD thy God giveth thee.
Exodus 20:12

Fifth Commandment   130. O

Thou shalt not kill.
Exodus 20:13
Sixth Commandment   131. O

Thou shalt not commit adultery.
Exodus 20:14
Seventh Commandment   132. O

Thou shalt not steal.
Exodus 20:15
Eighth Commandment   133. O

**Thou shalt not bear false witness
against thy neighbour.**
Exodus 20:16
Ninth Commandment   134. O

**Thou shalt not covet thy neighbour's house, thou shalt not
covet thy neighbour's wife, nor his manservant, nor his
maidservant, nor his ox, nor his ass, nor any thing
that is thy neighbour's.**
Exodus 20:17
Tenth Commandment   135. O

**For this is the love of God, that we keep his
commandments: and his commandments are not grievous.**
1 John 5:3   136. O

**For I am not ashamed of the gospel of Christ: for it is
the power of God unto salvation ...**
Romans 1:16   137. O

**In whom we have redemption through his blood,
even the forgiveness of sins:**
Colossians 1:14   138. O

Therefore being justified by faith, we have peace with God through our Lord Jesus Christ:

Romans 5:1

139. O

If God be for us, who can be against us?

Romans 8:31

140. O

... seek those things which are above, where Christ sitteth on the right hand of God.

Colossians 3:1

141. O

But if we walk in the light, as he is in the light, we have fellowship one with another, and the blood of Jesus Christ his Son cleanseth us from all sin.

1 John 1:7

142. O

Himself took our infirmities, and bare our sicknesses.

Jesus Christ, Matthew 8:17

143. O

But God commendeth his love toward us, in that, while we were yet sinners, Christ died for us.

Romans 5:8 144. O

37 Yea, they sacrificed their sons and their daughters unto devils, 38 and shed innocent blood, even the blood of their sons and of their daughters, whom they sacrificed unto the idols of Canaan: and the land was polluted with blood.

Psalm 106:37-38

145. O   146. O

How much more shall the blood of Christ, who through
the eternal Spirit offered himself without spot to God,
purge your conscience from dead works
to serve the living God?
Hebrews 9:14
147. O

4 (For the weapons of our warfare are not carnal, but
mighty through God to the pulling down of strong holds;)
5 Casting down imaginations, and every high thing
that exalteth itself against the knowledge of God,
and bringing into captivity every thought
to the obedience of Christ;
2 Corinthians 10:4-5
148. O   149. O

8 But unto the Son he saith, Thy throne, O God,
is for ever and ever: a sceptre of righteousness
is the sceptre of thy kingdom.
9 Thou hast loved righteousness, and hated iniquity...
Hebrews 1:8-9
150. O   151. O

Death and life are in the power of the tongue:
and they that love it shall eat the fruit thereof.
Proverbs 18:21
152. O

And be not conformed to this world: but be ye transformed
by the renewing of your mind, that ye may prove what is
that good, and acceptable, and perfect, will of God.
Romans 12:2
153. O

**For he hath made him to be sin for us, who knew no sin;
that we might be made the righteousness of God in him.**
2 Corinthians 5:21
154. O

**Behold, I give unto you power to tread on serpents
and scorpions, and over all the power of the enemy:
and nothing shall by any means hurt you.**
Jesus Christ, Luke 10:19
155. O

Have faith in God.
Jesus Christ, Mark 11:22
156. O

✑

**If any man will come after me,
let him deny himself, and take up his cross, and follow me.**
Jesus Christ, Matthew 16:24
157. O

**...all these blessings shall come on thee, and overtake thee,
if thou shalt hearken unto the voice of the LORD thy God.**
Deuteronomy 28:2
158. O

**... how then can I do this great wickedness,
and sin against God?**
Genesis 39:9 159. O

**If ye abide in me, and my words abide in you,
ye shall ask what ye will, and it shall be done unto you.**
John 15:7
160. O

... But if thou do that which is evil, be afraid; for he beareth
not the sword in vain: for he is the minister of God, a
revenger to execute wrath upon him that doeth evil.
Romans 13:4

161. O

There is no fear in love; but perfect love
casteth out fear: because fear hath torment.
He that feareth is not made perfect in love.
1 John 4:18 162. O

Be not afraid, only believe.
Jesus Christ, Mark 5:36

163. O

For God sent not his Son into the world to condemn the
world; but that the world through him might be saved.
John 3:17

164. O

He that believeth on him is not condemned:
but he that believeth not is condemned already,
because he hath not believed in the name
of the only begotten Son of God.
John 3:18

165. O

A soft answer turneth away wrath:
but grievous words stir up anger.
Proverbs 15:21 166. O

For what is a man profited, if he shall gain
the whole world, and lose his own soul?
or what shall a man give in exchange for his soul?
Jesus Christ, Matthew 16:26 167. O

33

2 **In my Father's house are many mansions: if it were not
so, I would have told you. I go to prepare a place for you.**
3 **And if I go and prepare a place for you,
I will come again, and receive you unto myself;
that where I am, there ye may be also.**
Jesus Christ, John 14:2-3
168. O   169. O

**For the preaching of the cross is to them that perish
foolishness; but unto us which are saved it is
the power of God.**
1 Corinthians 1:18
170. O

ॐ

**Neither is there salvation in any other:
for there is none other name under heaven
given among men, whereby we must be saved.**
Acts 4:12 171. O

**Commit thy way unto the LORD;
trust also in him; and he shall bring it to pass.**
Psalm 37:5 172. O

**Who is he that overcometh the world,
but he that believeth that Jesus is the Son of God?**
1 John 5:5 173. O

**For the word of God is quick, and powerful, and sharper
than any twoedged sword, piercing even to the dividing
asunder of soul and spirit, and of the joints and marrow,
and is a discerner of the thoughts and intents of the heart.**
Hebrews 4:12 174. O

18 **Flee fornication. ...**

19 **What? know ye not that your body is the temple of the Holy Ghost which is in you, which ye have of God, and ye are not your own?**
1 Corinthians 6:18-19
175. O   176. O

... as long as he sought the LORD, God made him to prosper.
2 Chronicles 26:5
177. O

... Follow me, and I will make you fishers of men.
Jesus Christ, Matthew 4:19
178. O

Surely goodness and mercy shall follow me all the days of my life ...
Psalm 23:6
179. O

So God created man in his own image, in the image of God created he him; male and female created he them.
Genesis 1:27 *180. O*

The effectual fervent prayer of a righteous man availeth much.
James 5:16 *181. O*

And it shall be, if thou do at all forget the Lord thy God, and walk after other gods, and serve them, and worship them, I testify against you this day that ye shall surely perish.
Deuteronomy 8:19
182. O

**If there be a controversy between men, and they come
unto judgment, that the judges may judge them;
then they shall justify the righteous,
and condemn the wicked.**
Deuteronomy 25:1
183. O

6 **... judges, Take heed what ye do: for ye judge not for
man, but for the LORD, who is with you in the judgment.
7 Wherefore now let the fear of the LORD be upon you;
take heed and do it: for there is no iniquity with the LORD
our God, nor respect of persons, nor taking of gifts.**
2 Chronicles 19:6-7
184. O   185. O

**Now unto him that is able to do
exceeding abundantly above all that we ask or think ...**
Ephesians 3:20
186. O

ॐ

Who against hope believed in hope ...
Romans 4:18
187. O

**But he was wounded for our transgressions, he was
bruised for our iniquities: the chastisement of our peace
was upon him; and with his stripes we are healed.**
Isaiah 53:5
188. O

15 **Love not the world, neither the things that are in the world. If any man love the world, the love of the Father is not in him.** 16 **For all that is in the world, the lust of the flesh, and the lust of the eyes, and the pride of life, is not of the Father, but is of the world.**

1 John 2:15-16

189. O   190. O

1 **Bless the LORD, O my soul: and all that is within me, bless his holy name.** 2 **Bless the LORD, O my soul, and forget not all his benefits:** 3 **Who forgiveth all thine iniquities; who healeth all thy diseases;** 4 **Who redeemeth thy life from destruction; who crowneth thee with lovingkindness and tender mercies;**

Psalm 100:1-4

191. O   192. O   193. O   194. O

38 **For I am persuaded, that neither death, nor life, nor angels, nor principalities, nor powers, nor things present, nor things to come,** 39 **nor height, nor depth, nor any other creature, shall be able to separate us from the love of God, which is in Christ Jesus our Lord.**

Romans 8:38-39

195. O   196. O

He sent his word, and healed them, and delivered them from their destructions.

Psalm 107:20

197. O

**As far as the east is from the west,
so far hath he removed our transgressions from us.**
Psalm 103:12

198. O

... greater is he that is in you, than he that is in the world.
1 John 5:4

199. O

୶

**The LORD is my light and my salvation;
whom shall I fear? the LORD is the strength
of my life; of whom shall I be afraid?**
Psalm 27:1

200. O

My Bible Verses

ℰ

Write other Scriptures you memorize here to have your verses in one place. More Bible verses to consider memorizing are: Psalm 91, 1 Corinthians 13, Galatians 5:19-21, Ephesians 3:17-19, Matthew 28:19-20, Matthew 11:28-30, Philippians 3:13-14, Isaiah 54:17, Psalm 2:10-12, 2 Thessalonians 3:10, 2 John 10-11, Colossians 1:15, Revelation 21:4, Acts 1:8, 1 Peter 3:15, 1 Corinthians 15:58, Ephesians 6:13 to have all of Ephesians 6:11-18 memorized, Isaiah 9:6, 2 Chronicles 16:9, Psalm 1, Romans 8, and James 1. To glorify God, you can memorize and learn new Scriptures continuously.

_____

_____

_____

_____

_____

_____

_____

_____

_____

_____

_____

_____

_____

_____

_____

_____

_____

_____

_____

_____

_____

_____

_____

_____

_____

_____

_____

_____

_____

_____

_____

_____

_____

_____

_____

_____

_____

_____

_____

_____

_____

_____

_____

_____

_____

_____

_____

_____

_____

_____

_____

_____

_____

_____

_____

My Bible Verses

_____

_____

_____

_____

_____

_____

_____

_____

_____

_____

_____

_____

_____

_____

_____

_____

_____

_____

_____

_____

_____

_____

_____

_____

_____

_____

_____

_____

_____

_____

_____

_____

_____

_____

_____

_____

_____

_____

_____

_____

_____

_____

_____

_____

_____

My Bible Verses

_____

_____

_____

_____

_____

_____

_____

_____

_____

_____

_____

_____

_____

_____

_____

_____

_____

_____

_____

_____

_____

_____

Promise Book

❧

Here is an encouraging Bible Promise Book with the memory verses to strengthen your faith for all your needs. You can find the Scriptures by topic. This also helps you memorize the Word of God.

❧ *Salvation* ❧

For all have sinned, and come short of the glory of God;
Romans 3:23 2.

For the wages of sin is death; but the gift of God is eternal life through Jesus Christ our Lord.
Romans 6:23 3.

But God commendeth his love toward us, in that, while we were yet sinners, Christ died for us.
Romans 5:8 144.

For God so loved the world, that he gave his only begotten Son, that whosoever believeth in him should not perish, but have everlasting life. *Jesus Christ, John 3:16* 4.

I am the way, the truth, and the life: no man cometh unto the Father, but by me. *Jesus Christ, John 14:6* 6.

Except a man be born again, he cannot see the kingdom of God.
Jesus Christ, John 3:3 8.

30 **... Sirs, what must I do to be saved?**
31 **And they said, Believe on the Lord Jesus Christ, and thou shalt be saved, and thy house.** *Acts 16:30-31* 34. 35.

9 **That if thou shalt confess with thy mouth the Lord Jesus,
and shalt believe in thine heart that God hath raised him
from the dead, thou shalt be saved.**
10 **For with the heart man believeth unto righteousness;
and with the mouth confession is made unto salvation.**
Romans 10:9-10 44. 45.

8 **For by grace are ye saved through faith;
and that not of yourselves: it is the gift of God:**
9 **Not of works, lest any man should boast.**
Ephesians 2:8- 9 80. 81.

**Neither is there salvation in any other:
for there is none other name under heaven
given among men, whereby we must be saved.**
Acts 4:12 171.

**Therefore if any man be in Christ,
he is a new creature: old things are passed away;
behold, all things are become new.**
2 Corinthians 5:17 108.

❧ *Forgiveness of Sins* ❧

**If we confess our sins, he is faithful and just to forgive us
our sins, and to cleanse us from all unrighteousness.**
1 John 1:9 7.

**My little children, these things write I unto you, that ye sin
not. And if any man sin, we have an advocate with the
Father, Jesus Christ the righteous:**
1 John 2:1 43.

**In whom we have redemption through his blood,
even the forgiveness of sins:**
Colossians 1:14 138.

**But God commendeth his love toward us,
in that, while we were yet sinners, Christ died for us.**
Romans 5:8 144.

**But if we walk in the light, as he is in the light, we have
fellowship one with another, and the blood of Jesus Christ
his Son cleanseth us from all sin.**
1 John 1:7 142.

**For he hath made him to be sin for us, who knew no sin;
that we might be made the righteousness of God in him.**
2 Corinthians 5:21 154.

**Therefore being justified by faith, we have peace with God
through our Lord Jesus Christ:**
Romans 5:1 139.

If you are not a Christian see the Salvation verses.

✌ *God* ✌

In the beginning God created the heaven and the earth.
Genesis 1:1 1.

**The LORD is gracious, and full of compassion;
slow to anger, and of great mercy.**
Psalm 145:8 5.

**But God commendeth his love toward us,
in that, while we were yet sinners, Christ died for us.**
Romans 5:8 144.

But the Comforter, which is the Holy Ghost, whom the Father will send in my name, he shall teach you all things, and bring all things to your remembrance, whatsoever I have said unto you.
Jesus Christ, John 14:26 77.

The fear of the LORD is the beginning of wisdom: and the knowledge of the holy is understanding.
Proverbs 9:10 49.

For the LORD is our judge, the LORD is our lawgiver, the LORD is our king; he will save us.
Isaiah 33:22 56.

And it shall be, if thou do at all forget the Lord thy God, and walk after other gods, and serve them, and worship them, I testify against you this day that ye shall surely perish.
Deuteronomy 8:19 182.

Have faith in God.
Jesus Christ, Mark 11:22 156.

❧ Jesus Christ ❧

I am the light of the world: he that followeth me shall not walk in darkness, but shall have the light of life.
Jesus Christ, John 8:12 19.

I am the resurrection, and the life:
he that believeth in me,
though he were dead, yet shall he live:
Jesus Christ, John 11:25 37.

The thief cometh not, but for to steal, and to kill,
and to destroy: I am come that they might have life,
and that they might have it more abundantly.
John 10:10 83

In whom we have redemption through his blood,
even the forgiveness of sins:
Colossians 1:14 138.

8 But unto the Son he saith, Thy throne, O God,
is for ever and ever: a sceptre of righteousness
is the sceptre of thy kingdom.
9 Thou hast loved righteousness, and hated iniquity...
Hebrews 1:8-9 150. 151.

Therefore being justified by faith, we have peace with God
through our Lord Jesus Christ:
Romans 5:1 139.

Neither is there salvation in any other:
for there is none other name under heaven
given among men, whereby we must be saved.
Acts 4:12 171.

But he was wounded for our transgressions, he was
bruised for our iniquities: the chastisement of our peace
was upon him; and with his stripes we are healed.
Isaiah 53:5 188.

For God sent not his Son into the world to condemn the
world; but that the world through him might be saved.
John 3:17 164.

He that believeth on him is not condemned:
but he that believeth not is condemned already,
because he hath not believed in the name
of the only begotten Son of God.
John 3:18 165.

✑ *Hope* ✑

Being confident of this very thing,
that he which hath begun a good work in you
will perform it until the day of Jesus Christ:
Philippians 1:6 16.

And we know that all things work together
for good to them that love God...
Romans 8:28 69.

Now the God of hope fill you with all joy and peace
in believing, that ye may abound in hope,
through the power of the Holy Ghost.
Romans 15:13 103.

I will never leave thee, nor forsake thee.
Hebrews 13:5 20.

If God be for us, who can be against us?
Romans 8:31 140.

... with God all things are possible.
Jesus Christ, Mark 10:27 64.

I am the light of the world: he that followeth me
shall not walk in darkness, but shall have the light of life.
Jesus Christ, John 8:12 19.

2 In my Father's house are many mansions: if it were not so, I would have told you. I go to prepare a place for you.
3 And if I go and prepare a place for you,
I will come again, and receive you unto myself;
that where I am, there ye may be also.
Jesus Christ, John 14:2-3 168. 169.

... greater is he that is in you, than he that is in the world.
1 John 5:4 199.

Who against hope believed in hope ...
Romans 4:18 187.

Now unto him that is able to do
exceeding abundantly above all that we ask or think ...
Ephesians 3:20 186.

✑ *Assurance of Salvation* ✑

These things have I written unto you that believe
on the name of the Son of God; that ye may know
that ye have eternal life, and that ye may believe on
the name of the Son of God.
1 John 5:13 63.

As far as the east is from the west,
so far hath he removed our transgressions from us.
Psalm 103:12 198.

30 ... Sirs, what must I do to be saved?
31 And they said, Believe on the Lord Jesus Christ,
and thou shalt be saved, and thy house.
Acts 16:30-31 34. 35.

❧ *Accepted* ❧

... he hath made us accepted in the beloved.
Ephesians 1:6 28.

**There is therefore now no condemnation
to them which are in Christ Jesus,
who walk not after the flesh, but after the Spirit.**
Romans 8:1 41.

❧ *Supply of Needs* ❧

**... my God shall supply all your need
according to his riches in glory by Christ Jesus.**
Philippians 4:19 9.

**But seek ye first the kingdom of God, and his
righteousness; and all these things shall be
added unto you.**
Matthew 6:33 68.

**Delight thyself also in the LORD;
and he shall give thee the desires of thine heart.**
Psalm 37:4 94.

14 **And this is the confidence that we have in him, that, if
we ask any thing according to his will, he heareth us:**
15 **And if we know that he hear us, whatsoever we ask,
we know that we have the petitions
that we desired of him.**
1 John 5:14-15 121. 122.

...all these blessings shall come on thee, and overtake thee,
if thou shalt hearken unto the voice of the LORD thy God.
Deuteronomy 28:2 158.

✑ *Edify* ✑

Let no corrupt communication proceed out of your mouth,
but that which is good to the use of edifying,
that it may minister grace unto the hearers.
Ephesians 4:29 116.

✑ *Fear* ✑

For God hath not given us the spirit of fear;
but of power, and of love, and of a sound mind.
2 Timothy 1:7 11.

For I the LORD thy God will hold thy right hand,
saying unto thee, Fear not; I will help thee.
Isaiah 41:13 24.

For ye have not received the spirit of bondage again to
fear; but ye have received the Spirit of adoption, whereby
we cry, Abba, Father.
Romans 8:15 88.

There is no fear in love; but perfect love
casteth out fear: because fear hath torment.
He that feareth is not made perfect in love.
1 John 4:18 162.

Be not afraid, only believe.
Jesus Christ, Mark 5:36 163.

... when they began to sing and to praise,
the LORD set ambushments against
the children of Ammon, Moab, and mount Seir,
which were come against Judah; and they were smitten.
2 Chronicles 20:22 65.

The LORD is my light and my salvation; whom shall I fear?
the LORD is the strength of my life; of whom shall I be
afraid? *Psalm 27:1* 200.

The LORD is my light and my salvation;
whom shall I fear? the LORD is the strength
of my life; of whom shall I be afraid?
Psalm 27:1 200.

❧ *Grace* ❧

8 **For by grace are ye saved through faith;
and that not of yourselves: it is the gift of God:**
9 **Not of works, lest any man should boast.**
Ephesians 2:8- 9 80. 81.

Let no corrupt communication proceed out of your mouth,
but that which is good to the use of edifying,
that it may minister grace unto the hearers.
Ephesians 4:29 116. O

❧ *Relationships* ❧

If it be possible, as much as lieth in you,
live peaceably with all men.
Romans 12:18 106.

But if we walk in the light, as he is in the light, we have
fellowship one with another, and the blood of Jesus Christ
his Son cleanseth us from all sin.
1 John 1:7 142.

҉ Finances, Need ҉

... my God shall supply all your need
according to his riches in glory by Christ Jesus.
Philippians 4:19 9.

But seek ye first the kingdom of God, and his
righteousness; and all these things shall be added
unto you. *Matthew 6:33* 68.

But without faith it is impossible to please him:
for he that cometh to God must believe that he is,
and that he is a rewarder of them that diligently seek him.
Hebrews 11:6 86.

... as long as he sought the LORD, God made him
to prosper. *2 Chronicles 26:5* 177.

҉ The Lord Delivers Me, God's Protection ҉

9 Because thou hast made the LORD, which is my refuge,
ever the most High, thy habitation;
10 There shall no evil befall thee,
neither shall any plague come nigh thy dwelling.
Psalm 91:9-10 98. 99.

For in the time of trouble he shall hide me
in his pavilion: in the secret of his tabernacle
shall he hide me; he shall set me up upon a rock.
Psalm 27:5 115.

The LORD is my light and my salvation;
whom shall I fear? the LORD is the strength
of my life; of whom shall I be afraid?
Psalm 27:1 200.

✺ *Evangelism* ✺

... Follow me, and I will make you fishers of men.
Jesus Christ, Matthew 4:19 178.

See the Salvation Bible verses.

✺ *Faith, Answered Prayer* ✺

For we walk by faith, not by sight:
2 Corinthians 5:7 101.

Now faith is the substance of things hoped for,
the evidence of things not seen.
Hebrews 11:1 107.

But without faith it is impossible to please him:
for he that cometh to God must believe that he is,
and that he is a rewarder of them that diligently seek him.
Hebrews 11:6 86.

Who against hope believed in hope ...
Romans 4:18 187.

And when ye stand praying, forgive,
if ye have ought against any: that your Father also
which is in heaven may forgive you your trespasses.
Jesus Christ, Mark 11:25 32.

... whosoever shall say unto this mountain,
Be thou removed, and be thou cast into the sea; and shall
not doubt in his heart, but shall believe that those things
which he saith shall come to pass; he shall have
whatsoever he saith.
Jesus Christ, Mark 11:23 89.

What things soever ye desire, when ye pray,
believe that ye receive them, and ye shall have them.
Jesus Christ, Mark 11:24 90.

14 And this is the confidence that we have in him, that, if
we ask any thing according to his will, he heareth us:
15 And if we know that he hear us, whatsoever we ask,
we know that we have the petitions
that we desired of him.
1 John 5:14-15 121. 122.

If ye abide in me, and my words abide in you,
ye shall ask what ye will, and it shall be done unto you.
John 15:7 160.

Ask, and it shall be given you; seek, and ye shall find;
knock, and it shall be opened unto you:
Jesus Christ, *Matthew 7:7*
109. O

... with God all things are possible.
Jesus Christ, Mark 10:27 64.

Have faith in God. *Jesus Christ, Mark 11:22* 156.

**The effectual fervent prayer
of a righteous man availeth much.**
James 5:16 181.

✿ *Speech* ✿

**Let no corrupt communication proceed out of your mouth,
but that which is good to the use of edifying,
that it may minister grace unto the hearers.**
Ephesians 4:29 116.

**Let the words of my mouth, and the meditation of my
heart, be acceptable in thy sight, O LORD, my strength,
and my redeemer.** *Psalm 19:14* 117.

**Death and life are in the power of the tongue:
and they that love it shall eat the fruit thereof.**
Proverbs 18:21 152.

**A soft answer turneth away wrath: but grievous words
stir up anger.** *Proverbs 15:21* 166.

✿ *New Life in Christ* ✿

**Therefore if any man be in Christ,
he is a new creature: old things are passed away;
behold, all things are become new.**
2 Corinthians 5:17 108.

**For I am not ashamed of the gospel of Christ: for it is
the power of God unto salvation ...**
Romans 1:16 137.

❧ Mercy ❧

**The LORD is gracious, and full of compassion;
slow to anger, and of great mercy.**
Psalm 145:8 5.

**Surely goodness and mercy shall follow me
all the days of my life ...**
Psalm 23:6 179.

❧ Seek God ❧

**... they entered into a covenant to seek the LORD God
of their fathers with all their heart
and with all their soul;**
2 Chronicles 15:12 46.

**But seek ye first the kingdom of God, and his
righteousness; and all these things
shall be added unto you.**
Matthew 6:33 68.

**If my people, which are called by my name,
shall humble themselves, and pray, and seek my face,
and turn from their wicked ways; then will I hear from
heaven, and will forgive their sin, and will heal their land.**
2 Chronicles 7:14 48.

**... as long as he sought the LORD,
God made him to prosper.**
2 Chronicles 26:5 177.

❧ *Fruit of the Spirit* ❧

22 **But the fruit of the Spirit is love, joy, peace, longsuffering, gentleness, goodness, faith,** 23 **meekness, temperance: against such there is no law.**
Galatians 5:22-23 26. 27.

❧ *The Cross* ❧

For the preaching of the cross is to them that perish foolishness; but unto us which are saved it is the power of God.
1 Corinthians 1:18 170.

In whom we have redemption through his blood, even the forgiveness of sins:
Colossians 1:14 138.

How much more shall the blood of Christ, who through the eternal Spirit offered himself without spot to God, purge your conscience from dead works to serve the living God?
Hebrews 9:14 147.

❧ *Healing* ❧

… for I am the LORD that healeth thee.
Exodus 15:26 84.

… by whose stripes ye were healed.
1 Peter 2:24 85.

Himself took our infirmities, and bare our sicknesses.
Jesus Christ, Matthew 8:17 143.

9 **Because thou hast made the LORD, which is my refuge,**
even the most High, thy habitation;
10 **There shall no evil befall thee,**
neither shall any plague come nigh thy dwelling.
Psalm 91:9-10 98. 99.

Behold, I give unto you power to tread on serpents
and scorpions, and over all the power of the enemy:
and nothing shall by any means hurt you.
Jesus Christ, Luke 10:19 155.

But he was wounded for our transgressions, he was
bruised for our iniquities: the chastisement of our peace
was upon him; and with his stripes we are healed.
Isaiah 53:5 188.

He sent his word, and healed them,
and delivered them from their destructions.
Psalm 107:20 197.

1 **Bless the LORD, O my soul: and all that is**
within me, bless his holy name.
2 **Bless the LORD, O my soul, and forget not all his benefits:**
3 **Who forgiveth all thine iniquities;**
who healeth all thy diseases;
4 **Who redeemeth thy life from destruction;**
who crowneth thee with lovingkindness
and tender mercies;
Psalm 100:1-4 191. 192. 193. 194.

❧ *Victory Over Sin* ❧

Submit yourselves therefore to God. Resist the devil, and he will flee from you. *James 4:7* 18.

There hath no temptation taken you but such as is common to man: but God is faithful, who will not suffer you to be tempted above that ye are able; but will with the temptation also make a way to escape, that ye may be able to bear it.
1 Corinthians 10:13 38.

Likewise reckon ye also yourselves to be dead indeed unto sin, but alive unto God through Jesus Christ our Lord.
Romans 6:11 31.

... how then can I do this great wickedness, and sin against God? *Genesis 39:9* 159.

My little children, these things write I unto you, that ye sin not. And if any man sin, we have an advocate with the Father, Jesus Christ the righteous:
1 John 2:1 43.

Thy word have I hid in mine heart, that I might not sin against thee. *Psalm 119:11* 118.

❧ *Don't Worry, Supplication* ❧

Casting all your care upon him; for he careth for you.
1 Peter 5:7 104.

And we know that all things work together for good to them that love God... *Romans 8:28* 69.

6 **Be careful for nothing; but in every thing**
by prayer and supplication with thanksgiving
let your requests be made known unto God.
7 **And the peace of God, which passeth all understanding,**
shall keep your hearts and minds through Christ Jesus.
Philippians 4:6-7 119. 120.

14 **And this is the confidence that we have in him, that, if**
we ask any thing according to his will, he heareth us:
15 **And if we know that he hear us, whatsoever we ask,**
we know that we have the petitions
that we desired of him.
1 John 5:14-15 121. 122. O

Commit thy way unto the LORD;
trust also in him; and he shall bring it to pass.
Psalm 37:5 172.

Fear not: for they that be with us
are more than they that be with them.
2 Kings 6:16 105.

✑ *Courage* ✑

Be strong and of a good courage; be not afraid,
neither be thou dismayed: for the LORD thy God is with
thee whithersoever thou goest.
Joshua 1:9 42.

Fear not: for they that be with us
are more than they that be with them.
2 Kings 6:16 105.

66

✌ Raise Godly Generations, Ministry ✌

For I am not ashamed of the gospel of Christ: for it is the power of God unto salvation ...
Romans 1:16 137.

As for me, this *is* my covenant with them, saith the LORD; My spirit that *is* upon thee, and my words which I have put in thy mouth, shall not depart out of thy mouth, nor out of the mouth of thy seed, nor out of the mouth of thy seed's seed, saith the LORD, from henceforth and for ever.
Isaiah 59:21 96.

For the preaching of the cross is to them that perish foolishness; but unto us which are saved it is the power of God.
1 Corinthians 1:18 170.

✌ Liberty ✌

... where the Spirit of the Lord is, there is liberty.
2 Corinthians 3:17 78.

... the glorious liberty of the children of God.
Romans 8:21 79

✌ Strength ✌

I can do all things through Christ ...
Philippians 4:13 10.

**But they that wait upon the LORD shall renew their
strength; they shall mount up with wings as eagles;
they shall run, and not be weary;
and they shall walk, and not faint.**
Isaiah 40:31 61.

❧ The Love of God ❧

38 **For I am persuaded, that neither death, nor life,
nor angels, nor principalities, nor powers,
nor things present, nor things to come,**
39 **nor height, nor depth, nor any other creature,
shall be able to separate us from the love of God,
which is in Christ Jesus our Lord.**
Romans 8:38-39 195. 196.

**For God so loved the world, that he gave his only begotten
Son, that whosoever believeth in him should not perish,
but have everlasting life.**
Jesus Christ, John 3:16 4.

**But God commendeth his love toward us,
in that, while we were yet sinners, Christ died for us.**
Romans 5:8 144.

❧ Power ❧

**But they that wait upon the LORD shall renew their
strength; they shall mount up with wings as eagles;
they shall run, and not be weary;
and they shall walk, and not faint.**
Isaiah 40:31 61.

For God hath not given us the spirit of fear;
but of power, and of love, and of a sound mind.
2 Timothy 1:7 11.

❧ *Praise* ❧

... when they began to sing and to praise,
the LORD set ambushments against
the children of Ammon, Moab, and mount Seir,
which were come against Judah; and they were smitten.
2 Chronicles 20:22 65.

❧ *Victory Over the Devil, Spiritual Warfare* ❧

Submit yourselves therefore to God. Resist the
devil, and he will flee from you. *James 4:7* 18.

The thief cometh not, but for to steal, and to kill, and to
destroy: I am come that they might have life, and that they
might have it more abundantly. *Jesus Christ, John 10:10* 83.

Behold, I give unto you power to tread on serpents
and scorpions, and over all the power of the enemy:
and nothing shall by any means hurt you.
Jesus Christ, Luke 10:19 155.

9 Because thou hast made the LORD, which is my refuge,
even the most High, thy habitation;
10 There shall no evil befall thee,
neither shall any plague come nigh thy dwelling.
Psalm 91:9-10 98. 99.

**Put on the whole armour of God, that ye may be able
to stand against the wiles of the devil.**
Ephesians 6:11 70.

**For we wrestle not against flesh and blood, but against
principalities, against powers, against the rulers of the
darkness of this world, against spiritual wickedness
in high places.** *Ephesians 6:12* 71.

14 **Stand therefore, having your loins girt about with truth,
and having on the breastplate of righteousness;**
15 **And your feet shod with the preparation
of the gospel of peace;**
16 **Above all, taking the shield of faith, wherewith ye shall
be able to quench all the fiery darts of the wicked.**
17 **And take the helmet of salvation,
and the sword of the Spirit, which is the word of God:**
18 **Praying always with all prayer and supplication
in the Spirit, and watching thereunto with all perseverance
and supplication for all saints;**
Ephesians 6:14-18 72. 73. 74. 75. 76.

4 **(For the weapons of our warfare are not carnal, but
mighty through God to the pulling down of strong holds;)**
5 **Casting down imaginations, and every high thing
that exalteth itself against the knowledge of God, and
bringing into captivity every thought
to the obedience of Christ;**
2 Corinthians 10:4-5 148. 149.

... **greater is he that is in you, than he that is in the world.**
1 John 5:4 199.

❧ Covenant Christian Nation ❧

**For the LORD is our judge, the LORD is our lawgiver,
the LORD is our king; he will save us.**
Isaiah 33:22 56.

Blessed is the nation whose God is the LORD ...
Psalm 33:12 25.

**If my people, which are called by my name,
shall humble themselves, and pray, and seek my face,
and turn from their wicked ways; then will I hear from
heaven, and will forgive their sin, and will heal their land.**
2 Chronicles 7:14 48.

**... they entered into a covenant to seek the LORD God
of their fathers with all their heart and with all their soul;**
2 Chronicles 15:12 46.

**And the king stood in his place, and made a covenant
before the LORD, to walk after the LORD, and to keep his
commandments, and his testimonies, and his statutes,
with all his heart, and with all his soul, to perform the
words of the covenant which are written in this book.**
2 Chronicles 34:31 95.

❧ Representatives Fear God, Christian Nation Government ❧

**... provide out of all the people able men, such as fear God,
men of truth, hating covetousness; and place such over
them, to be rulers...** *Exodus 18:21* 59.

**He that ruleth over men must be just,
ruling in the fear of God.**
2 Samuel 23:3 60.

... the LORD hath sought him a man after his own heart ...
1 Samuel 13:14 110.

We ought to obey God rather than men. *Acts 5:29* 55.

❧ *Judgment and Justice* ❧

**If there be a controversy between men, and they come
unto judgment, that the judges may judge them; then they
shall justify the righteous, and condemn the wicked.**
Deuteronomy 25:1 183.

6 **... judges, Take heed what ye do: for ye judge not for
man, but for the LORD, who is with you in the judgment.**
7 **Wherefore now let the fear of the LORD be upon you;
take heed and do it: for there is no iniquity with the LORD
our God, nor respect of persons, nor taking of gifts.**
2 Chronicles 19:6-7 184. 185.

**... But if thou do that which is evil, be afraid; for he beareth
not the sword in vain: for he is the minister of God, a
revenger to execute wrath upon him that doeth evil.**
Romans 13:4 161.

❧ *Children* ❧

Children, obey your parents in the Lord: for this is right.
Ephesians 6:1 12.

2 **Honour thy father and mother; (which is the first commandment with promise;)** *3* **That it may be well with thee, and thou mayest live long on the earth.**
Ephesians 6:2-3 *13. 14.*

❧ *Direction and Guidance* ❧

5 **Trust in the LORD with all thine heart; and lean not unto thine own understanding.** *6* **In all thy ways acknowledge him, and he shall direct thy paths.**
Proverbs 3:5-6 *21. 22.*

If any of you lack wisdom, let him ask of God, that giveth to all men liberally, and upbraideth not; and it shall be given him.
James 1:5 *50.*

A soft answer turneth away wrath: but grievous words stir up anger. *Proverbs 15:21* *166.*

This book of the law shall not depart out of thy mouth; but thou shalt meditate therein day and night, that thou mayest observe to do according to all that is written therein: for then thou shalt make thy way prosperous, and then thou shalt have good success.
Joshua 1:8 *97.*

❧ *The Word of God* ❧

For this is the love of God, that we keep his commandments: and his commandments are not grievous.
1 John 5:3 *136.*

16 **All scripture is given by inspiration of God,**
and is profitable for doctrine, for reproof,
for correction, for instruction in righteousness:
17 **That the man of God may be perfect,**
throughly furnished unto all good works.
2 Timothy 3:16-17 113. 114.

For the word of God is quick, and powerful, and sharper
than any twoedged sword, piercing even to the dividing
asunder of soul and spirit, and of the joints and marrow,
and is a discerner of the thoughts and intents of the heart.
Hebrews 4:12 174.

And the king stood in his place, and made a covenant
before the LORD, to walk after the LORD, and to keep his
commandments, and his testimonies, and his statutes,
with all his heart, and with all his soul, to perform the
words of the covenant which are written in this book.
2 Chronicles 34:31 95.

This book of the law shall not depart out of thy mouth;
but thou shalt meditate therein day and night,
that thou mayest observe to do according to all that is
written therein: for then thou shalt make thy way
prosperous, and then thou shalt have good success.
Joshua 1:8 97.

Thy word have I hid in mine heart,
that I might not sin against thee.
Psalm 119:11 118.

∽ Trust God ∼

Be still, and know that I am God:
Psalm 46:10 17.

5 **Trust in the LORD with all thine heart;**
and lean not unto thine own understanding.
6 **In all thy ways acknowledge him,**
and he shall direct thy paths.
Proverbs 3:5-6
21. O   22. O

Commit thy way unto the LORD;
trust also in him; and he shall bring it to pass.
Psalm 37:5 172.

∽ Pride ∼

15 **Love not the world, neither the things that are**
in the world. If any man love the world, the love of the
Father is not in him. 16 **For all that is in the world, the lust**
of the flesh, and the lust of the eyes, and the pride of life,
is not of the Father, but is of the world.
1 John 2:15-16 189. 190.

A soft answer turneth away wrath:
but grievous words stir up anger.
Proverbs 15:21 166.

∽ Truth ∼

... the truth shall make you free.
John 8:32 62.

75

I am the way, the truth, and the life:
no man cometh unto the Father, but by me.
Jesus Christ, John 14:6 6.

❧ *Biblical Success* ❧

This book of the law shall not depart out of thy mouth;
but thou shalt meditate therein day and night,
that thou mayest observe to do according to all that is
written therein: for then thou shalt make thy way
prosperous, and then thou shalt have good success.
Joshua 1:8 97.

I am crucified with Christ: nevertheless, I live;
yet not I, but Christ liveth in me: and the life which I now
live in the flesh I live by the faith of the Son of God,
who loved me, and gave himself for me.
Galatians 2:20 36.

For the love of money is the root of all evil:
1 Timothy 6:10 123.

...all these blessings shall come on thee, and overtake thee,
if thou shalt hearken unto the voice of the LORD thy God.
Deuteronomy 28:2 158.

As far as the east is from the west,
so far hath he removed our transgressions from us.
Psalm 103:12 198.

For God sent not his Son into the world to condemn the
world; but that the world through him might be saved.
John 3:17 164.

He that believeth on him is not condemned:
but he that believeth not is condemned already,
because he hath not believed in the name
of the only begotten Son of God.
John 3:18 165.

❧ *Peace* ❧

Thou wilt keep him in perfect peace, whose mind is stayed
on thee: because he trusteth in thee.
Isaiah 26:3 39.

6 Be careful for nothing; but in every thing
by prayer and supplication with thanksgiving
let your requests be made known unto God.
7 And the peace of God, which passeth all understanding,
shall keep your hearts and minds through Christ Jesus.
Philippians 4:6-7 119. 120.

Now the God of hope fill you with all joy and peace
in believing, that ye may abound in hope,
through the power of the Holy Ghost.
Romans 15:13 103.

Come unto me, all ye that labour and are heavy laden, and
I will give you rest. *Matthew 11:28* 112.

❧ *Forgive* ❧

And when ye stand praying, forgive,
if ye have ought against any: that your Father also
which is in heaven may forgive you your trespasses.
Jesus Christ, Mark 11:25 32.

And be ye kind one to another, tenderhearted,
forgiving one another, even as God
for Christ's sake hath forgiven you.
Ephesians 4:32 23.

If it be possible, as much as lieth in you, live peaceably
with all men. *Romans 12:18* 106.

Blessed are the peacemakers:
for they shall be called the children of God.
Jesus Christ, Matthew 5:9 87.

✍ *Shame* ✍

If we confess our sins, he is faithful and just to forgive us
our sins, and to cleanse us from all unrighteousness.
1 John 1:9 7.

There is therefore now no condemnation to them
which are in Christ Jesus, who walk not after the flesh,
but after the Spirit.
Romans 8:1 41.

For he hath made him to be sin for us, who knew no sin;
that we might be made the righteousness of God in him.
2 Corinthians 5:21 154.

✍ *Love God* ✍

And thou shalt love the Lord thy God with all thy heart,
and with all thy soul, and with all thy mind, and with all thy
strength: this is the first commandment.
First Commandment, Jesus Christ, Mark 12:30 57.

For thou shalt worship no other god:
for the LORD, whose name is Jealous, is a jealous God:
Exodus 34:14 67.

... as for me and my house, we will serve the LORD.
Joshua 24:15 100.

And it shall be, if thou do at all forget the Lord thy God,
and walk after other gods, and serve them,
and worship them, I testify against you this day
that ye shall surely perish.
Deuteronomy 8:19
182.

For this is the love of God, that we keep his
commandments: and his commandments are not grievous.
1 John 5:3 136.

❧ *Longsuffering, Patience* ❧

22 **But the fruit of the Spirit is love, joy, peace,**
longsuffering, gentleness, goodness, faith,
23 **meekness, temperance: against such there is no law.**
Galatians 5:22-23 26. 27.

... let every man be swift to hear, slow to speak,
slow to wrath: *James 1:19* 47.

❧ *Healing of the Soul,*
Healing of a Broken Heart ❧

He restoreth my soul:
Psalm 23:3 29.

He healeth the broken in heart,
and bindeth up their wounds. *Psalm 147:3* 30.

How much more shall the blood of Christ, who through
the eternal Spirit offered himself without spot to God,
purge your conscience from dead works
to serve the living God? *Hebrews 9:14* 147.

For God hath not given us the spirit of fear;
but of power, and of love, and of a sound mind.
2 Timothy 1:7 11.

Come unto me, all ye that labour
and are heavy laden, and I will give you rest.
Matthew 11:28 112.

❧ *Death* ❧

I am the resurrection, and the life: he that believeth in me,
though he were dead, yet shall he live:
Jesus Christ, John 11:25 37.

2 In my Father's house are many mansions: if it were not
so, I would have told you. I go to prepare a place for you.
3 And if I go and prepare a place for you,
I will come again, and receive you unto myself;
that where I am, there ye may be also.
Jesus Christ, John 14:2-3 168. 169.

❧ *Comfort* ❧

I will never leave thee, nor forsake thee.
Hebrews 13:5 20.

For I the LORD thy God will hold thy right hand, saying unto thee, Fear not; I will help thee. *Isaiah 41:13* 24.

But the Comforter, which is the Holy Ghost, whom the Father will send in my name, he shall teach you all things, and bring all things to your remembrance, whatsoever I have said unto you.
Jesus Christ, John 14:26 77.

For I the LORD thy God will hold thy right hand, saying unto thee, Fear not; I will help thee.
Isaiah 41:13 24.

If God be for us, who can be against us?
Romans 8:31 140.

Now unto him that is able to do exceeding abundantly above all that we ask or think ...
Ephesians 3:20 186.

Thou wilt keep him in perfect peace, whose mind is stayed on thee: because he trusteth in thee. *Isaiah 26:3* 39.

∾ *Love One Another* ∾

And the second is like, namely this, Thou shalt love thy neighbour as thyself.
Second Commandment, Jesus Christ, Mark 12:31 58

Let no corrupt communication proceed out of your mouth, but that which is good to the use of edifying, that it may minister grace unto the hearers.
Ephesians 4:29 116.

And now abideth faith, hope, charity, these three;
but the greatest of these *is* charity.
1 Corinthians 13:13 111.

‧ *Glorify God* ‧

... the LORD hath sought him a man after his own heart ...
1 Samuel 13:14 110.

Let your light so shine before men, that they may see your
good works, and glorify your Father which is in heaven.
Jesus Christ, Matthew 5:16 40.

And whatsoever ye do, do it heartily, as to the Lord,
and not unto men; *Colossians 3:23* 66.

Let the words of my mouth, and the meditation of my
heart, be acceptable in thy sight, O LORD, my strength,
and my redeemer. *Psalm 19:14* 117.

‧ *Righteousness* ‧

8 But unto the Son he saith, Thy throne, O God,
is for ever and ever: a sceptre of righteousness
is the sceptre of thy kingdom.
9 Thou hast loved righteousness, and hated iniquity...
Hebrews 1:8-9 150. 151.

If my people, which are called by my name,
shall humble themselves, and pray, and seek my face,
and turn from their wicked ways; then will I hear from
heaven, and will forgive their sin, and will heal their land.
2 Chronicles 7:14 48.

❧ God Created Male and Female ❧

So God created man in his own image, in the image of God
created he him; male and female created he them.
Genesis 1:27 180.

The woman shall not wear that which pertaineth unto a
man, neither shall a man put on a woman's garment:
for all that do so are abomination unto the LORD thy God.
Deuteronomy 22:5 82.

Thou shalt not lie with mankind, as with womankind:
it is abomination.
Leviticus 18:22 53.

❧ God's Will ❧

... seek those things which are above,
where Christ sitteth on the right hand of God.
Colossians 3:1 141.

14 And this is the confidence that we have in him, that, if
we ask any thing according to his will, he heareth us:
15 And if we know that he hear us, whatsoever we ask,
we know that we have the petitions
that we desired of him.
1 John 5:14-15 121. 122.

And be not conformed to this world: but be ye transformed
by the renewing of your mind, that ye may prove what is
that good, and acceptable, and perfect, will of God.
Romans 12:2 153.

If any man will come after me,
let him deny himself, and take up his cross, and follow me.
Jesus Christ, Matthew 16:24 157.

Commit thy way unto the LORD;
trust also in him; and he shall bring it to pass.
Psalm 37:5 172.

୰ *Bless the Lord* ୰

1 Bless the LORD, O my soul: and all that is within me, bless his holy name. *2* Bless the LORD, O my soul, and forget not all his benefits: *3* Who forgiveth all thine iniquities; who healeth all thy diseases; *4* Who redeemeth thy life from destruction; who crowneth thee with lovingkindness and tender mercies; *Psalm 100:1-4* 191. 192. 193. 194.

୰ *Anger* ୰

... let every man be swift to hear, slow to speak,
slow to wrath: *James 1:19* 47.

The LORD is gracious, and full of compassion;
slow to anger, and of great mercy.
Psalm 145:8 5.

୰ *What to Think, Thoughts* ୰

... whatsoever things are true, whatsoever things are honest, whatsoever things are just, whatsoever things are pure, whatsoever things are lovely, whatsoever things are of good report; if there be any virtue, and if there be any praise, think on these things. *Philippians 4:8* 33.

Let the words of my mouth, and the meditation of my
heart, be acceptable in thy sight, O LORD, my strength,
and my redeemer.
Psalm 19:14 117.

For God hath not given us the spirit of fear;
but of power, and of love, and of a sound mind.
2 Timothy 1:7 11.

❧ Sexual Purity ❧

18 **Flee fornication. ...**
19 **What? know ye not that your body is the temple of the
Holy Ghost which is in you, which ye have of God, and ye
are not your own?**
1 Corinthians 6:18-19 175. 176.

Thou shalt not lie with mankind,
as with womankind: it is abomination.
Leviticus 18:22 53.

❧ Christian Home, Family ❧

Wives, submit yourselves unto your own husbands,
as unto the Lord. *Ephesians 5:22* 51.

Husbands, love your wives, even as Christ
also loved the church, and gave himself for it;
Ephesians 5:25 52.

Train up a child in the way he should go:
and when he is old, he will not depart from it.
Proverbs 22:6 54.

**Blessed are the peacemakers:
for they shall be called the children of God.**
Jesus Christ, Matthew 5:9 87.

... as for me and my house, we will serve the LORD.
Joshua 24:15 100.

**As for me, this *is* my covenant with them, saith the LORD;
My spirit that *is* upon thee, and my words which I have put
in thy mouth, shall not depart out of thy mouth, nor out of
the mouth of thy seed, nor out of the mouth of thy seed's
seed, saith the LORD, from henceforth and for ever.**
Isaiah 59:21 96.

**And be ye kind one to another, tenderhearted,
forgiving one another, even as God for Christ's sake
hath forgiven you.** *Ephesians 4:32* 23.

✑ *Christian Life* ✑

... as for me and my house, we will serve the LORD.
Joshua 24:15 100.

We ought to obey God rather than men.
Acts 5:29 55.

**And whatsoever ye do, do it heartily, as to the Lord,
and not unto men;** *Colossians 3:23* 66.

**I am crucified with Christ: nevertheless, I live;
yet not I, but Christ liveth in me: and the life which I now
live in the flesh I live by the faith of the Son of God,
who loved me, and gave himself for me.**
Galatians 2:20 36.

22 **But the fruit of the Spirit is love, joy, peace,
longsuffering, gentleness, goodness, faith,**
23 **meekness, temperance: against such there is no law.**
Galatians 5:22-23 26. 27.

**... seek those things which are above,
where Christ sitteth on the right hand of God.**
Colossians 3:1 141.

18 **Flee fornication. ...**
19 **What? know ye not that your body is the temple
of the Holy Ghost which is in you, which ye have of God,
and ye are not your own?**
1 Corinthians 6:18-19 175. 176.

**Thou shalt not lie with mankind,
as with womankind: it is abomination.**
Leviticus 18:22 53.

**The woman shall not wear that which pertaineth unto a
man, neither shall a man put on a woman's garment:
for all that do so are abomination unto the LORD thy God.**
Deuteronomy 22:5 82.

10 **There shall not be found among you any one that
maketh his son or his daughter to pass through the fire, or
that useth divination, or an observer of times,
or an enchanter, or a witch,**
11 **or a charmer, or a consulter with familiar spirits,
or a wizard, or a necromancer.**
12 **For all that do these things are an abomination unto the
LORD: and because of these abominations the LORD thy**

God doth drive them out from before thee.
Deuteronomy 18:10-12 *91. 92. 93.*

37 **Yea, they sacrificed their sons and**
their daughters unto devils,
38 **and shed innocent blood, even the blood of their sons**
and of their daughters, whom they sacrificed unto the idols
of Canaan: and the land was polluted with blood.
Psalm 106:37-38 *145. 146.*

If any man will come after me,
let him deny himself, and take up his cross, and follow me.
Jesus Christ, Matthew 16:24 *157.*

15 **Love not the world, neither the things that are**
in the world. If any man love the world,
the love of the Father is not in him.
16 **For all that is in the world, the lust of the flesh,**
and the lust of the eyes, and the pride of life,
is not of the Father, but is of the world.
1 John 2:15-16 *189. 190.*

Pray without ceasing.
1 Thessalonians 5:17 *102.*

❧ *Hell* ❧

For what is a man profited, if he shall gain
the whole world, and lose his own soul?
or what shall a man give in exchange for his soul?
Jesus Christ, Matthew 16:26 *167.*

❧ Ten Commandments ❧

I am the LORD thy God ...

Exodus 20:2

Preface of our Lawgiver   124.

Thou shalt have no other gods before me.

Exodus 20:3

First Commandment   125.

**4 Thou shalt not make unto thee any graven image,
or any likeness of any thing that is in heaven above,
or that is in the earth beneath, or that is in
the water under the earth:
5 Thou shalt not bow down thyself to them, nor serve
them: for I the LORD thy God am a jealous God...**

Exodus 20:4-5

Second Commandment   126. 127.

**Thou shalt not take the name of the LORD thy God in vain;
for the LORD will not hold him guiltless
that taketh his name in vain.**

Exodus 20:7

Third Commandment   128.

8 Remember the sabbath day, to keep it holy.

Exodus 20:8

Fourth Commandment   129.

**Honour thy father and thy mother:
that thy days may be long upon the land
which the LORD thy God giveth thee.**

Exodus 20:12

Fifth Commandment   130.

Thou shalt not kill.
Exodus 20:13
Sixth Commandment   131.

Thou shalt not commit adultery.
Exodus 20:14
Seventh Commandment   132.

Thou shalt not steal.
Exodus 20:15
Eighth Commandment   133.

Thou shalt not bear false witness against thy neighbour.
Exodus 20:16
Ninth Commandment   134.

Thou shalt not covet thy neighbour's house, thou shalt not covet thy neighbour's wife, nor his manservant, nor his maidservant, nor his ox, nor his ass, nor any thing that is thy neighbour's.
Exodus 20:17
Tenth Commandment   135.

✺ *Keep God's Commandments* ✺

And the king stood in his place, and made a covenant before the LORD, to walk after the LORD, and to keep his commandments, and his testimonies, and his statutes, with all his heart, and with all his soul, to perform the words of the covenant which are written in this book.
2 Chronicles 34:31   95.

❧ *Holiness* ❧

We ought to obey God rather than men.
Acts 5:29 55.

Likewise reckon ye also yourselves to be dead indeed unto sin, but alive unto God through Jesus Christ our Lord.
Romans 6:11 31.

Be ye holy; for I am holy.
1 Peter 1:16 15.

Submit yourselves therefore to God.
Resist the devil, and he will flee from you.
James 4:7 18.

My little children, these things write I unto you, that ye sin not. And if any man sin, we have an advocate with the Father, Jesus Christ the righteous:
1 John 2:1 43.

Let the words of my mouth, and the meditation of my heart, be acceptable in thy sight, O LORD, my strength, and my redeemer. *Psalm 19:14* 117.

15 **Love not the world, neither the things that are in the world. If any man love the world, the love of the Father is not in him.**
16 **For all that is in the world, the lust of the flesh, and the lust of the eyes, and the pride of life, is not of the Father, but is of the world.**
1 John 2:15-16 189. 190.

Thy word have I hid in mine heart,
that I might not sin against thee.
Psalm 119:11 118.

⚜ Wisdom ⚜

The fear of the LORD is the beginning of wisdom: and the
knowledge of the holy is understanding.
Proverbs 9:10 49.

If any of you lack wisdom, let him ask of God,
that giveth to all men liberally,
and upbraideth not; and it shall be given him.
James 1:5 50.

This book of the law shall not depart out of thy mouth;
but thou shalt meditate therein day and night,
that thou mayest observe to do according to all that is
written therein: for then thou shalt make thy way
prosperous, and then thou shalt have good success.
Joshua 1:8 97.

Commit thy way unto the LORD;
trust also in him; and he shall bring it to pass.
Psalm 37:5 172.

⚜ Free of the Past ⚜

How much more shall the blood of Christ, who through
the eternal Spirit offered himself without spot to God,
purge your conscience from dead works
to serve the living God?
Hebrews 9:14 147.

Therefore if any man be in Christ, he is a new creature: old things are passed away; behold, all things are become new.
2 Corinthians 5:17 108.

❧ *Victory In Jesus* ❧

Who is he that overcometh the world,
but he that believeth that Jesus is the Son of God?
1 John 5:5 173.

Surely goodness and mercy shall follow me
all the days of my life ...
Psalm 23:6 179.

❧